Your Body:

3. Feeding and Digestion

Dr. Gwynne Vevers

Illustrated by Sarah Pooley

LOTHROP, LEE & SHEPARD BOOKS
New York

OTHER TITLES IN THIS SERIES
Skin and Bone
Blood and Lungs
Muscles and Movement

Text copyright © 1984 by Gwynne Vevers
Illustrations © 1984 by Sarah Pooley
First published in Great Britain in 1984 by The Bodley Head
Printed in the United States of America.
First U.S. Edition   1   2   3   4   5   6   7   8   9   10
Library of Congress Cataloging in Publication Data
Vevers, Gwynne, 1916-
    Your body.
    Includes index.
    Contents: 1. Skin and Bone—2. Blood and lungs— [etc.]—4. Muscles and movement.
    1. Body, Human—Juvenile literature. 2. Body, Human. I. Pooley, Sarah, ill. II. Title.
QP37.V48 1983   612   83-18757
ISBN 0-688-02830-6
ISBN 0-688-02831-4 (lib. bdg.)

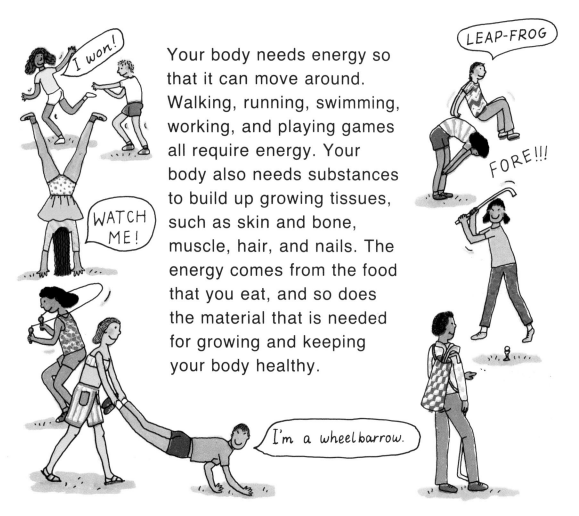

Your body needs energy so that it can move around. Walking, running, swimming, working, and playing games all require energy. Your body also needs substances to build up growing tissues, such as skin and bone, muscle, hair, and nails. The energy comes from the food that you eat, and so does the material that is needed for growing and keeping your body healthy.

There are many different kinds of foods, and they are mostly mixtures of three main substances known as carbohydrates, fats, and proteins.

Carbohydrates are starchy and sugary foods, such as bread and potatoes, cakes and cookies. These provide a lot of energy.

Fats are greasy or oily substances like butter and margarine. They are also found in egg yolk and in peanuts. Fats also provide plenty of energy.

Proteins are the substances used to build up the body. You get them from meat and fish, peas and beans, and the white (albumen) of eggs.

The body also needs liquids, such as water, milk, and fruit juices, and very small quantities of substances known as vitamins.

The amount of energy you get from each kind of food is measured in calories. For example, one gram of carbohydrate or protein has 4 calories, but one gram of a fat such as butter supplies 9 calories.

73 Calories

A cup of cocoa

50 Calories

An apple

300 Calories–or more!

An ice cream sundae

300 Calories

A can of baked beans

65 Calories

A slice of bread with no butter

THE FOOD CANAL

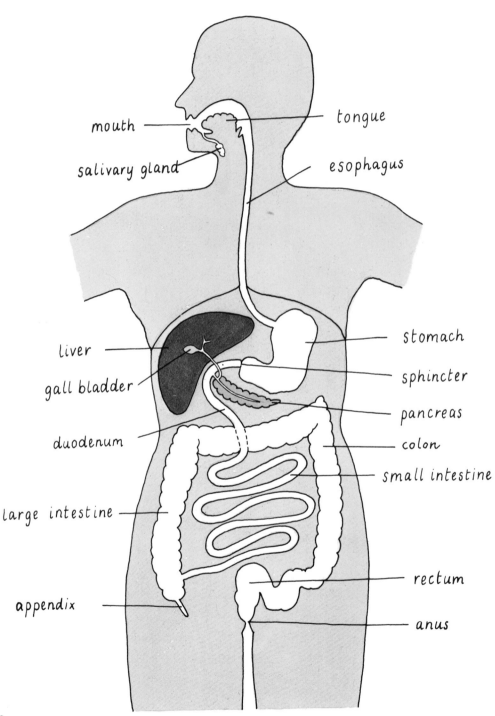

mouth

tongue

salivary gland

esophagus

liver

stomach

gall bladder

sphincter

pancreas

duodenum

colon

small intestine

large intestine

rectum

appendix

anus

Food can only be used for energy or bodybuilding after it has been broken down in different parts of the food canal, which is also called the alimentary tract, and absorbed into the bloodstream, which then distributes it to the different parts of your body. This process is known as digestion.

When you drink water or milk or juice, you swallow it immediately, since there is no need to chew it. But when you eat solid food, you chew it with your teeth and, with help from the tongue, it becomes mixed with saliva or spit in your mouth.

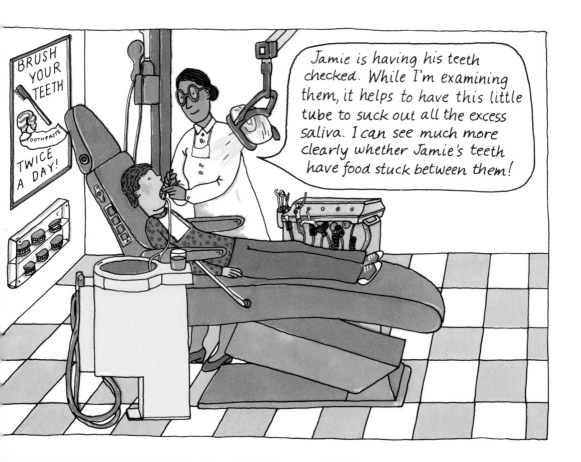

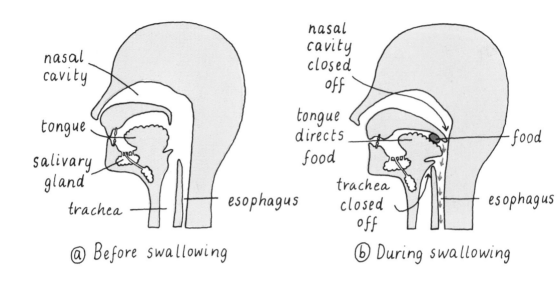

ⓐ Before swallowing

ⓑ During swallowing

As you swallow the chewed food, the slippery saliva helps it to slide down into your stomach through a tube called the esophagus. The saliva comes from three pairs of glands that open into your mouth. More saliva is produced when you see or smell some tasty food, such as ice cream, chocolate cake, or French fries.

The saliva contains an enzyme, which is a substance that helps to digest the food. The saliva changes some of the starch in bread, potatoes, and some other foods into a kind of sugar. If you chew a small piece of unbuttered bread for several minutes, it becomes sweet.

A SALIVARY ENZYME PERFORMING A MAGICAL TRICK

Your stomach is a muscular bag, and its lining contains about 35 million glands, which produce acid and two more enzymes, known as pepsin and rennin. When the stomach muscles contract, the food is moved around and mixed with the digestive juice from the tiny glands.

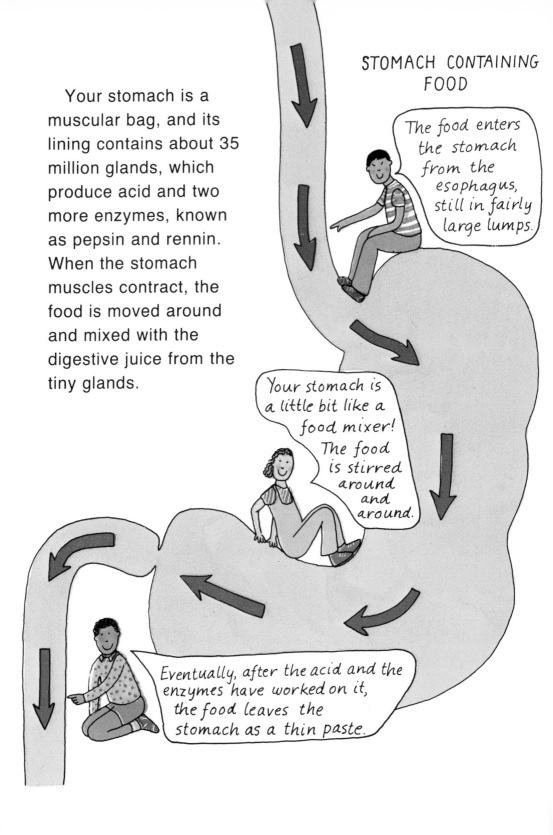

STOMACH CONTAINING FOOD

The enzyme pepsin starts the job of breaking down some of the protein in the food you have chewed and swallowed. The other enzyme, rennin, makes milk set or coagulate, turning it into a curd. This helps babies and young mammals to digest milk slowly. If the milk did not set to a curd, it would go almost straight through your body before you could absorb any goodness from it.

By the time the stomach enzymes and the acid have worked on the food, it has become almost liquid, like very thin paste. The stomach acid also kills off harmful bacteria.

The paste moves on into the small intestine, passing through a narrow opening, or sphincter, at the bottom of your stomach. When this sphincter is open, the paste passes into the first part of the small intestine. This is a tube, about 12 inches (30 cm) long, known as the duodenum.

In the duodenum the food paste receives still more digestive juice from a gland called the pancreas.

The juice from the pancreas contains three main enzymes: one helps to break down proteins, one acts on fats, and one works on carbohydrates. The duodenum also receives bile from the liver. Bile acts like a detergent, breaking up fats into smaller and smaller particles that pass farther down the food canal.

The food is moved or squeezed on by muscles in the walls of the small intestine. The duodenum itself produces even more digestive juice, and this finishes the digestion of the fats, carbohydrates, and proteins. By now the food has become semiliquid and can be absorbed through the walls of the small intestine. There it passes into the bloodstream, which carries it to your liver and on to different parts of your body. The liver also stores sugar in a form called glycogen, which can be used when necessary to provide energy.

The amount of sugar in the blood is kept at a constant level by the action of a substance called insulin, which is produced by the pancreas. Some people do not have enough insulin to keep their blood sugar at the right level, and so they have a disease known as diabetes. They have to have insulin shots daily and must stay on a diet with reduced sugar and other carbohydrates. Fortunately, they still can live full and active lives.

There are so many villi in your small intestine that it would be impossible to count them all!

Most of the job of food absorption takes place in the small intestine, which has walls with enormous numbers of tiny fingerlike projections called villi. You would only be able to see these if you were to look at a piece of the small intestine through a microscope.

The villi are shaped like your fingers!

1, 2, 3, 4, 5, 6...

7, 8, 9, 10, 11, 12...

This is a villus. The name for more than one villus is villi.

These are blood vessels supplying the villi.

This is part of the small intestine as seen under the microscope.

Proteins from food contain amino acids. These build up your body tissues. They are necessary not just for strong muscles, hair, nails, and skin, but also for kidney and liver cells and the bone marrow that makes red blood cells.

Fats from food are absorbed as a kind of liquid and then built up again as a store of energy in fat cells all over the body. Babies and young children have a thick layer of fat under the skin, and this insulates them against losing body heat. Adults who live in a cold climate, such as Eskimos, also need a fatty layer to help maintain body temperature.

Fat forms a protective sheath to cover all the vital and delicate nerves in the body. It fills bony gaps, such as the space behind the eyeballs, and gives rounded contours to the body. Fat also surrounds the kidneys.

After food material has been absorbed by the body, anything that is left over passes on from the small intestine to the large intestine.

Part of the large intestine, a section called the colon, has the job of removing water from the waste material.

By the time the waste has reached the bottom end of the large intestine, the rectum, it is more compact, fairly dry, and brown from bile pigments. From time to time this brownish waste, known as feces, is passed out of the body at the anus.

In humans the appendix is a small, fingerlike organ which branches off between the small and large intestines and is not useful to us.

Tony has just had his appendix out and is recovering in the hospital.

Yes, sometimes your appendix gets infected and gives you bad pains. But a simple operation makes you better again.

Hello.

We've brought him some grapes.

But in some animals, such as rabbits, the appendix is much larger, and it helps to digest the cellulose that makes up a large part of grass and other plant tissue.

RABBIT   HUMAN

Compare the size of the rabbit's appendix to the human's.

I need a big one because I eat grass and carrots.

Liquids that you drink, as well as water from food (cabbage and lettuce are full of water) pass into the bloodstream and on to the kidneys. Each kidney has a kind of filter, called the glomerulus, where the blood loses nearly all its excess water and other substances. The excess fluid passes into long, looped kidney tubules. Only the cells of the blood and the proteins are too big to escape through the glomerulus.

KIDNEY, CUT IN HALF

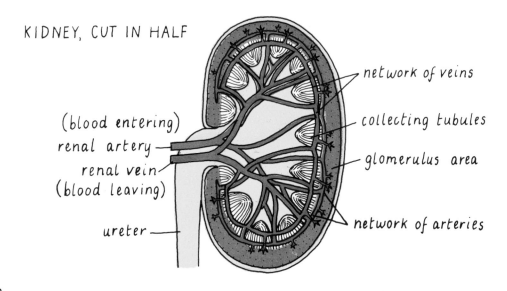

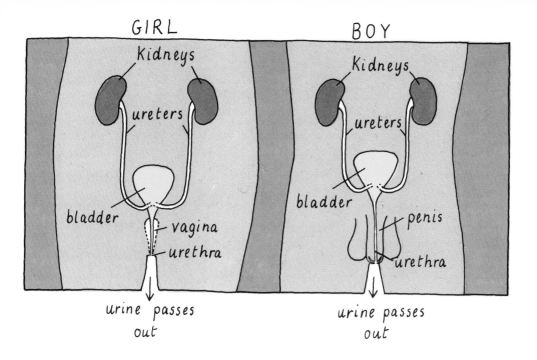

The fluid passes on down the tubules, where it becomes more concentrated. The tubules unite to form the ureters, and these pass the urine down to your bladder, where it is held and released at intervals.

Index

Page numbers in *italic type* indicate illustrations.